endorsements

Kimanzi Constable gets a BIG thumbs up for his book, *Are You Living or Existing?*—He goes beyond just delivering a highly inspiring book (which this very much is I might add) and also delivers real life strategies for taking your life from wishing & dreaming, to fully experiencing the truly rich & wondrous life that we're all born to live. Kimanzi is just like us all, he knows what it's like to want for more in life, but what makes him one heck of a special guy in my book is that he went beyond wishing for his life to be better, and took the necessary action that was required to bend it to fit the vision he had for himself. Now he's made it his life's work to help others do the same—this terrific book is going to help a lot of folks do just that."

Josh Hinds,
speaker & author of, *It's Your Life, LIVE BIG!*
www.JoshHinds.com

"I generally do not like books with titles like this one because they tend to be motivational/inspirational hyperbole.

Not Kimanzi's book. From the very start, he makes it clear what you'll have to do if you want to live your dreams, then takes you through a realistic timeframe of steps to get you focused, organized, and WORKING toward what you want. No hype. Just reality—What it really takes to get the job DONE."

Dagny Kight
Perisphere Publishing

"Do you dream of doing something great? We all do and so does Kimanzi Constable. In *Are You Living Or Existing?*, he shares his 9 step turnaround plan, and he knows what he's talking about. His life has been a living example of his plan in action as he's gone from bread-man to an international speaking sensation. You'll be able to apply his action steps to your life and begin to see huge changes. What are you waiting for?"

Joseph Lalonde,
Leadership writer at JMLalonde.com

"Too many people walk away from their passion with the negative belief that pursuing it would be unrealistic. Kimanzi has identified how moving toward our passion is not only possible but is the only option for having a life of purpose and meaning. A great example for all people who think they're stuck in the life they have now."

Dan Miller,
Author and Life Coach
(www.48Days.com)

"*Are Living or Existing* is a book that challenges you to not except less as your very best. What Kimanzi outlines in vivid detail is how to break your pattern of so called "normal" thinking, and focus on identifying what does and does not work. Then taking specific actions to create change and then build momentum. His book will enlighten, educate, and encourage you to be a better, happier and passionate person that helps others."

Darren Scott Monroe,
Info Marketer, Author and Speaker

"If you are ready to live a better life, buy this book! Kimanzi will take you, step-by-step, from where you are, to where you want to be."

Drew Tewell,
author of *The Dream Job Program*

Kimanzi Constable

are you
LIVING
or
existing?

9 steps to
change your life

Sound Wisdom

P.O. Box 310, Shippensburg, PA 17257-0310

For more information on foreign distribution, call 717-530-2122.

Reach us on the Internet: www.soundwisdom.com.

ISBN 13 TP: 978-1-937879-24-2

ISBN 13 Ebook: 978-1-937879-25-9

For Worldwide Distribution, Printed in the U.S.A.

1 2 3 4 5 6 7 8 / 16 15 14 13 12

disclaimer

I'm not a lawyer.

I'm not a doctor.

I'm not a personal trainer.

I'm not a financial planner.

I'm not a change expert.

I'm in the same boat as you, but I've decided to do something about it!

The information contained in this book is for informational purposes only.

I am not a lawyer or an accountant. Any legal or financial advice that I give is my opinion based on my own experience. You should always seek the advice of a professional before acting on something that I have published or recommended.

No part of this publication shall be reproduced, transmitted, or sold in whole or in part in any form, without the prior written consent of the author. All trademarks appearing in this book are the property of their respective owners.

Users of this book are advised to do their own due diligence when it comes to making business decisions and all

thank you

I want to thank my beautiful wife and lovely children for all their support and for putting up with me while I was writing this book.

I also want to give a big thank you to my supportive, uplifting, challenging group of friends, who are always motivating me to dream bigger and do more: Chaka Dillon El, William Haeflinger, and David Constable. Thank you guys for all that you do!

contents

Introduction:

Introduction:

What's the point?
Why change your life?
Why nine steps?
Who cares?

Have you ever had someone you know, or a loved one, suddenly die? If you have, the one thing that often sticks out the most is how short life is. It passes quicker than we think. If, Lord willing, you make it to a very ripe old age, what sort of life will you look back on from your deathbed? Did you "live" or did you "exist"? Will your memories be filled with all the amazing things that you did in your life, or will you remember the episodes of your favorite TV show? When you die, what will others say about you?

So you're pretty hardcore and you read this and say, "SO WHAT? I lived my life the way I wanted; I don't care what anyone else thinks." Hey, it's your prerogative to think that way, and if you're happy with your life, then more power to you! However, I have to ask you to be honest with yourself; are you really happy? Do you believe you can truly be happy?

If you're not happy with your life, and you want to make a change, then this is the right place. Realize that this book will not magically cure all your problems in life; I'm sorry, but I just don't have that ability. However, this book will not only give you a plan to change your life, but also teach you to enjoy the journey.

The same-old same-old gets old quick!

Do you go through each day feeling like you live in the matrix? You know what I'm talking about, don't you? You get up every day and pretty much do the same things: you go to a job you hate, you talk to coworkers you might not exactly care for, you look at the clock at work and can't wait for it to be over, only to come home and veg out in front of the TV...

This is what I mean by just existing. This kind of life gets old pretty fast!

When was the last time you did something new and exciting? Now you might hear the question and think, "I don't have money to do something new and exciting," but you don't need money. How about going for a brisk run through the park? How about taking your kids on a bike ride? How about reading a good book? Life has so much more to offer then sitting at home in front of that stupid TV or spending all day checking updates on social media!

You have that nagging sense in the back of your mind when you read this, don't you? That voice that is trying to tell you that what you're doing is the same-old same-old? It's time for a change, buddy. Why not give it a try and change things up a little bit, what could it hurt?

I want more for my life!

You might be living out your dreams right now, and if you are, kudos. I know it's a privilege just to be alive, so don't sit there and think I'm complaining; I'm not. What I'm talking about is the fact that God means for us to be happy and to live happy lives. He means for us to follow our dreams and encourage others to do that as well. What things have you dreamed of in your life? Are you at your dream job? Are you active with your kids every day? Do you read or write or do anything intellectual? Or do you get up, go to work, get home, and watch the latest prime-time shows all night? I think you see what I'm saying, and if you just don't have the energy to do anything because life feels overwhelming, then it's time for a change!

You want more because you deserve more, and God wants you to have more, so why are you hesitating? For myself, I'm tired of living in Wisconsin, for me being here is the same-old same-old. My wife and I have dreamed of retiring in Hawaii. Recently we realized, "Why do we want to go there when we're old and can't really enjoy it? Why wait?" We decided we want more, and God willing, by January of next year, we'll be out there living!

Even reading about this thought process makes me want to scream. Why do we hesitate to follow our dreams when the world has so much to offer us? Why can't we see what's right in front of our faces? How long will we live in fear of failure?

At some point you have to scream: ENOUGH!

Again I ask you, what more have you wanted from your life?

A nine-step plan

I designed this plan and this book based on the concept of taking nine steps to completely change your life. Although originally conceived as a nine-month plan, it can actually work in whatever time frame you want. We are taking one year to plan our move to Hawaii, to make sure all our ducks are in a row and we have a solid back-up plan. You might decide to make drastic changes, and it might take you less time–super cool!

I used nine months as my original timeframe in order to give you enough time to think things through, to write down a solid, step-by-step plan, and to have enough room to implement that plan. The amount of time doesn't matter so much; implementing the nine steps defined in this book will give you the vision and the means to see it through.

It's not a race, as you probably already know; you're striving to change your life, to move to somewhere new, to do something you've been thinking about all your life. Would it hurt to take nine steps to make sure you do things right?

Have you heard the expression, "good things come to those who wait?" This will be a nine-step marathon through a scenic journey made of anger, tiredness, struggles, happiness, victories, and sometimes losses. This has to be something you really want; you can't do it halfheartedly.

I want to be honest with you up front, and let you know the journey will be super-hard. You'll be going against things that are ingrained in your mind, and that won't be easy. You'll have to learn things you have probably never thought about before. Yes, this journey will be hard, but if you push through it and stick with it, I promise it will be worth the effort!

Use the principles in this book to help guide you with whatever changes you want to make, and let it be a resource for you! If you find the book helpful, pass it along; tell others to pick it up. I'm hoping to start a movement of people who are committed to radical change, and committed to helping others radically change!

the
DIFFERENCE
between
LIVING
and existing

The main difference between living and just existing is your attitude towards what you do, which affects how you do it and how you feel about your life.

Existing:

"I'm really not looking forward to work on Monday."

"I just don't have the energy to work out today."

"The kids have another play; didn't we just go to one?"

"I'm not going anywhere on my vacation, I'm going to stay home and catch up on sleep."

"I only have three years until retirement, so I'll do more things then."

Living:

"I can't wait for Monday because I'm going to help people."

"I had the best workout today; I felt like I could go another thirty minutes!"

"The kids only have seven events at school this year? Bummer, we'll have to come up with our own extra events."

"I just got back from a week in Mexico. That's four different countries we've gone to this year."

"I don't think I could ever retire from this business that I absolutely love."

Now to be fair you might not be able to go to four different countries because of finances; I get that, but could you afford to go if you stopped eating out all the time? I get that work life can be busy and hectic, and make you too tired to go to the play, but are you tired from doing a job that is meaningful and helps people? If not, why are you wasting your time?

"I got bills to pay." I get that, so do I, but is that all life is about, paying bills?

Look, don't go out and quit your job and move to Hawaii with no plan, that's stupid! The way my wife and I are doing it is to sit down, figure out our expenses, and save each week; we have a game plan, and you need one, too. If you develop a step-by-step plan, make it realistic, and stick to it, then in nine months or however long it takes, you'll be living out your dreams!

I hope you don't read this and think that this is "pie in the sky." People live out their dreams every day, and you can, too! Life is too short; we can't just exist anymore, WE HAVE TO LIVE!

I have talked to you a lot in this introduction because I want you to see exactly what this book is about; I want you to know the truth up front. If you're happy with your life then

I say congrats, and I hope you still read this book, just for a good read, and then maybe give it to someone you think could benefit from it.

There are too many of us just "existing," and it's time for us as a people to break this cycle!

Changing the
WORLD
Starts with
YOU!

*When I was young and free and my imagination
had no limits,
I dreamed of changing the world.
As I grew older and wiser I discovered the
world would not change –
So I shortened my sights somewhat and decided to
change only my country,
But it too seemed immovable.
As I grew into my twilight years,
in one last desperate attempt,
I settled for changing only my family, those closest to me,
But alas, they would have none of it.
And now I realize as I lie on my deathbed,
if I had only changed myself first,*

Then by example I might have changed my family,
From their inspiration and encouragement I would then
have been able to better my country,
And who knows, I might have even changed the world.

This is an inscription on the tomb of an Anglican bishop in Westminster Abbey.

I'm committed to the message I present in this book. I suspect that if you have read this far, that little voice in your head is whispering that you're in the right place; I hope you continue and start to believe. If you decide that extreme change is not for you, or you're not ready, then I wish you well, but please, *don't stand in your own way.*

The choice is now yours: do you move forward and make changes or do you just continue going down the same road? Only you can answer that!

Chapter 1:

Chapter 1:

Identify
Your Dreams
(First Step)

We will start our nine step journey to change your life by taking the first step: we need to figure out where we want to go. We need to identify the areas of our lives that we want to change, and formulate a plan of action. First we need to be sure we really want to make these changes; once we have figured out what things we want to change, we need a plan to achieve the goals we set. Think of this as establishing the basics.

Identify the things you truly want to change

You may be at a job that you like, where you have never had an issue with the work or the people, but one day or one week, everything goes wrong. Your boss is constantly yelling at you, you messed up three tasks, your coworkers are driving you bonkers--AAHH! All of this may happen and it may make you think, "I really want to quit and change jobs!" but do you really? You can have a bad week at a job you like; you just have to realize it's a bad week. If you made a change to a different job because of one bad week, you might ruin the rest of your life!

Maybe you are thinking about changing the way you behave as a parent to your kids? What if you have firmly believed in spanking but decide to make a change and use the grounding method? Your kids could see this and have a field day, and you may have "lost" them.

Do you really want to change your job, your style of parenting, or other parts of your life, or are you just going through a rough patch? You need to be very sure before you start this journey.

We all have bad experiences; the key is to figure out if they are one-time things, or if they will be repeating themselves over and over again. You have to be honest with yourself about what's going on, be honest about the changes you're thinking about making. If you're just having a bad day, then great, you don't need to make a change. But, don't lie to yourself anymore! If this is more than just a bad day, remember–the truth always has a way of finding you.

Identify the actions to make the changes

So, you have taken a little time and made sure you weren't just going through a rough patch. Now you have an idea of what you want to change. Take the baby steps to get started. You don't have to change overnight; you just have to move forward.

If you want to lose weight this year, you don't have to do it in a week; you might want to sign up for a gym membership, or take a walk. Take these baby steps that can lead to the bigger change. Identify these first steps for each of the areas you want to change. Be very specific!

Right now as you read this, can you think of something that you really want to change? I know you have one thing that's been nagging at you. What kind of baby steps can you take this week? What one specific thing can you do to make forward progress, so that at the end of the week you can say you made a change?

If you identify a change you want to make, and take a baby step to start on your journey of change, tell us all about it here: kimanziconstable.com.

There are not many things that you can learn overnight. It's the same way with making changes, as you already know. It may seem scary to think about changing certain aspects of your life; that's natural. Remember that many who have been where you are right now would tell you that making a change was the best decision of their life!

This is make-it-or-break-it time, right here and right now. You have thought about changing things; you may even have taken some action, but you never went all the way. Let's all agree: this time, we're going all the way.

Start making changes gradually

Two years ago I decided I wanted to change my weight, so I hit it very hard and lost 132 pounds. The problem was I didn't do it gradually. I would go to the gym for four hours a day, and I ate 1,200 calories a day. I lost the weight super-fast, but I was always tired, always cranky. I didn't do it gradually, so I missed out on learning some valuable lessons; as a result I gained all the weight back and more. Going slowly teaches you the importance of never going back to what you just changed. If you move too fast, you might end up hitting a bump, falling down, and getting so frustrated that you give up. Go slow; look at it as a marathon and not a sprint.

Remember that you are radically changing things, and you want the changes to stick with you forever; go slow and make sure you do it right. Modify your life in such a way that you won't have to go back and change your changes! By taking things gradually, you can see things more clearly, and deal with the "bumps" before you hit them!

You'll naturally be impatient, naturally want to steamroll forward. You can do that, and probably make some progress, but in the end you'll have missed the lessons, and then you will be blind to the things that are creeping back into your life. I didn't learn to moderate my workouts, so when I lost weight I had a false sense of security; I didn't know how much working out I needed to keep doing.

Even now, I'm learning from my mistake. You can learn from it too; make the effort to learn each lesson as we go through these steps together. Learn how to make changes gradually, learn what got you to where you were. Use this information to fight any attempts, by yourself or anyone else, to drag you back down. We're not going back there, right?

Enjoy the journey

We're always so quick to rush through things that we miss the best part, the thrill of the journey! I know it doesn't "feel" thrilling while you're running on a treadmill trying to lose weight–I've been there. However, it can be a thrill if you realize what the end result will be. As I discussed when I mentioned a death in the family, life is short; the journey and its struggles are part of the time we have left. That's why, even though life can seem like a struggle, just too hard to deal with, we have to look at each challenge as something to enjoy.

I don't want to lose you here because you think my method is unrealistic or pie in the sky, it's really not. Instead of focusing on all the negative parts and letting them discourage you, try to turn your life around, using new and different tools to help. It can be a thrill to listen to a great audio book while you are running, better yet an amazing podcast that will help you in other areas of your life. Life is *sooo* short; we have to take advantage and enjoy each little moment, because before you know it, they'll all be gone!

Remember when you were a kid, how much you truly enjoyed life? Everything was thrilling and exciting, always a new mystery and challenge to explore and figure out. Remember how even when you were bad and got grounded, you still found a way, even in your room, to make it an adventure? Now you're an adult, and I trust no one will ground you, but why can't you still have that thrill? Even when making hard changes you can find a way to enjoy the small victories as you get them. You can make this exercise of change into a mini-adventure, almost like when you were a kid. It's *in* you, I know it is; you just have to dig deep and find it. Are you willing?

If you can truly learn to savor each moment, learning how to have joy as you work your way through struggles, it will seem like you have created extra time in your life!

We spend a lot of time worrying and fretting over things that are out of our control, and that's time we could use to radically change our situation. One thing I say a lot in this book is that we can't afford to waste any time–it's the one thing we can't get back!

Reach out for support

Sometimes the road can be bumpy and rough, but with a little support from friends or loved ones, it will be bearable. I hope you have someone in your life that you can reach out to, someone to tell things honestly and completely. I hope you don't think of reaching out as a failure. We all need a little help every now and then.

At some of my darkest moments I've had to reach out for support from my close group of friends. Do you know how valuable a group like that can be? If you have a close group of friends that not only support you, but push you to do better, no one can stop you from taking over the world!

I've been blessed to have this very kind of group, and if you follow my website then you know who I'm talking about. Every day we talk about our progress on our dream jobs, and if we haven't made any progress, then we call each other out for any excuses we might be making.

Do you have a close group of friends that will do this for you?

I don't think I need to tell you that the people you hang around with affect the progress you make at certain tasks, and even what progress you make in your life. People will certainly have an effect on whether you succeed at making your radical changes. Do you remember when you were in high school and all the cool kids were the "troublemakers?" What did you do when you wanted to be considered cool? You hung out with the bad kids and you got into a lot of trouble. You didn't care because then you were considered a cool kid, right?

Besides being considered cool, did hanging out with those kids improve your grades, your attitude, or your future? I have to tell you it works the same way when you're older. If you hang out with bums, they'll eventually drag you down to their level. All their negative energy will rub off on you and start creeping into other areas of your life. Trust me—I know this from personal experience.

I wanted to hang out with the people I thought were "cool," those that went out of their way to be different from everyone else; I wanted to be like that. They hated "the system" and bashed everything, and that energy made me an angry person. Here's the thing that I've come to realize, though (maybe you know this already):

Just be yourself, and stop trying to be someone you're not to impress other people.

When you hang out with people who are trying to get ahead in life, people that put their kids' needs ahead of their own, you'll find that they want you to get ahead, too. Guys or gals that not only want to succeed, but also want you to succeed, are the support group that you need. You'll all do better, you'll all work harder, and you'll all influence each other to grow to unimaginable levels of success.

If you don't have a group like this, can you start one?

You may have to be the first among your friends to organize a group like this; you may have to be the first to make progress and push your friends to do the same. However, if you do it, and your friends respond, the results will blow your mind! This group should be there for you no matter what–anytime, anyplace. They have to be **REAL**!

I'm blessed to have an amazing, inspiring group of friends that even believe enough in me to write about parenting on my website; I appreciate them so much. We're good for each other, because we all push each other in positive directions; you need this in your life. Those you hang out with will affect all areas of your life, so choose wisely...

How nice is it when you go and work out with a friend? When I'm running with a friend of mine, I look over at him and instantly get a jolt of energy to keep running. That kind of support can be the difference between success and failure in your effort to change. It can be a push when you're just not feeling it; I can guarantee there will be days on this nine-step journey when you need that push.

Support from friends can push you to work harder at your changes, or it can be a shoulder to cry on if the journey has you worn down. It's not cowardly to reach out for support; it could be the difference between success and failure!

Before you start this nine-step journey, it's important that you identify those people who will be your support system. Who will be the people in your life that will be there for you, those you can call at any time day or night? Who will be the people who will come and work out with you, or help you research that new place you're thinking of moving to? Right now, today, figure out who those people will be.

Once you have figured out who these people are, call them, take them out to lunch, and tell them exactly what's going on. Tell them what you're trying to change, and tell them exactly what you expect them to do, how they can best help you out. Setting this up ahead of time will help you get ten steps ahead in your plan to radically change your life!

Look for the light at the end of the tunnel

Have you ever heard the expression, "Begin with the end in mind?" It's so accurate. If you can't see where you're going, how do you expect to get there? So many times we have tunnel vision, focusing only on the negatives, the hurdles or the bumps we will hit in the road. Open your eyes and see what the end result will be. Stop looking only at the here and now.

No matter what, don't give up. Look ahead and see what your change will look like once you've finished. Remember what's at stake and why you want to make these changes. It might seem impossible at times, it might take everything you've got, but stay strong and keep pushing forward. If you see that light at the end of the tunnel, it will help you not to trip or stop!

Begin with the end in mind. If you want to lose fifty pounds, go out and buy some new clothes that you'll be able to wear when you've accomplished that goal. Keep those "skinny" clothes in a prominent place and use them as an object of motivation.

If you want to move to Hawaii, print out a few pictures of the area where you want to live. When you're tempted to spend money on something stupid, look at the pictures and use that target as the reason to not spend the money, even if it's only a few cents.

If you can do this with all the changes you want to make in your life, if you can find an object to use as motivation to get you through the roughest times, you will make the changes. You're making the changes for a reason, and that reason is the end result; focus on that and nothing else!

Don't give up, don't give up!

You can make it a long way on your nine-step plan and still quit. You could even make it to six steps and still be tempted to give up–don't do it. Knowing what to change and how to change it isn't the hard part; what's hard is actually putting in the legwork.

I want you to be excited about this journey. This is going to be a radical transformation, so you have to be pumped. I want you to be motivated; I want you to want it so much that you could scream right now. However, you need to have a clear understanding of the hurdles and challenges you're going to face. You have to see the problems ahead, and have a game plan for how to deal with them.

If you can do this and face those things, you will win. No matter what happens and what is thrown at you, don't give up. Whether you're two days into your journey, or two days from reaching your goal, don't give up. Everyone who reads this book needs to say, right now, "We won't give up until we make radical, life-altering changes!"

Are you with me?

At the end of the day it all comes down to this: How much do you want it? Do you want to change your life more than you want to continue going down the same road? It all comes down to that desire burning deep in you.

Is it there? Will you finally give in and change your life? I pray that you do.

Chapter 2:

Chapter 2:

Getting Fit

(Second Step)

So, here we are in the second step of this journey to radically change our lives. Our first step was seriously sitting down and figuring out what changes we wanted to make. If you are reading this and haven't really figured those changes out, please go back; take time to figure them out and then come back. Really doing the first step will give you the best chance for success.

Now, it's time for us to move forward and make some progress. I know this is what you've been waiting for, so here we go! This step, our focus is on getting fit physically, emotionally, and mentally.

Some of you may be "skinny," others of you may think that you're okay with your emotions and your state of mind; it's time for a reality check. If you do already meet these criteria, then take some time to get ahead and tune things up a little more; use this step to do prep work for the rest of the journey.

As always though, be really honest with yourself. Do you have everything together, or are you good at covering things up? If you have a spouse or partner, ask them to honestly tell you how you're doing–you have to get to the truth. If you don't think you need any help with your physical or emotional or mental fitness, and you move forward only to find you did need that help, then everything you do will be in vain. What's the point of that?

If you aren't "fit" then take action to shape up

We will start with physical aspects because getting on a physical routine will help complement the other two areas. Do you exercise? If you aren't on any kind of a workout routine, it's time to get started. Even if you're "skinny," you still can be out of shape. When you walk up a long flight of stairs, are you winded? Being physically fit is about a lot more than your weight; it's having your body in peak condition, which gives you strength and energy for every other area of your life.

Now I don't want you to suddenly start hitting the gym for four hours a day; doing that will lead to a pretty quick burnout. As we discussed in the first chapter, we'll start with gradual change, and we'll savor the journey. We will lay out a step-by-step plan to get into peak physical condition. To start getting fit, I just want you to do some kind of exercise at least twice a week. Two times a week is not a lot of time; go twice a week, and try and make it at least a half-hour each time.

With physical fitness, what's important is not how much time you spend, but what you do in that time. You can go to the gym for three hours a day and do nothing. Do you go to the gym just to soak in the hot tub? Are you catching up with all your old buddies, instead of getting a good sweat? Even though we're starting with half an hour, make that the most intense half-hour of your week.

I'm not telling you to go out and get a sixty-nine-dollar-a-month gym membership; you can start off very simply by going for a brisk walk or run in your neighborhood. Many people assume that to be "really working out" you have to be a part of the newest, latest gym, but that's just not true. Working out is working out, no matter where it is, as long as you're doing some physical exercise. If you don't have the money right now, don't sweat it; start off at home or outside until you get the funds. Once you get enough money, if you feel so inclined, then you can join one of those gyms; there are benefits to them. Remember that in the end your changes are YOURS, so the choice of how you implement these changes is your choice.

You can also make little everyday adjustments to supplement your workouts. How about taking the stairs at work instead of the elevator? How about parking your car farther away from the store and taking a longer walk? Not only will that be great exercise, but it will reduce the chance of your car getting hit in the parking lot! Just doing the little things and going the extra mile will help you get physically fit in no time.

If at all possible, try to work out at the beginning of your day. You may think this will take away all your energy, but you'll actually have more. I deliver bread at two a.m. in the morning (makes you cringe, doesn't it?), and I started working out before work. Everyone told me I would be too tired to run my delivery route. They thought I would lose all of my energy, but they were wrong. I ached at first; yet, as I told you, once my body got adjusted I started to feel stronger. As my body got stronger, throughout each day, I found I had a tremendous amount of energy. Think about it: I was building my strength; I was building my energy levels with the workouts. Afterwards, I would take a nice refreshing shower, and for the rest of the day, my body would adjust and push me through work.

Getting your blood pumping, working out those different muscles right away in the morning, will work wonders for you. It will also give you the chance to put on some great motivating music or listen to an amazing podcast. Whatever you do, make sure that what you're watching or listening to is upbeat, inspiring, and motivational. Following this routine will give you some of the best days you've ever had at work or even in your everyday life.

The first hour of the day is the most important hour. Have you ever "woken up on the wrong side of the bed?" I know it's just an expression, but if you have a bad first hour, it usually ruins the whole day. Start your first hour with things that are going to be a positive push in the right direction.

I know I've emphasized personal choice, but do me a favor: if you have the ability, try working out each morning for two weeks. Some who are reading this might not be able to work out before work because of an unusual schedule, and that's understandable. If you do have the opportunity to try it out though, give it a chance. If it doesn't work for you, you can always go back to your usual routine. It doesn't hurt to give it a try, right?

At the very start of working out (if you weren't doing so already), you will feel some aches and pains. Your body is being exposed to movements it's probably never felt before, so it's totally natural to feel sore the next morning. You'll get used to it after a while. During this time of transition, plan on getting extra sleep. When you're sleeping your body has time to heal; make sure you give your body a little extra time to heal while adjusting. I know this might mean missing your favorite TV show, or maybe even take away from something important like hanging out with your kids, but you have to remember that this is a short-term side effect to a solution for long-term issues.

During this time, try not to use too many medicines to help with the pain. The point is to get fit while keeping your body fresh and clean. If you have extreme pain, you have to do what's right for you, and you certainly should consult a doctor first and foremost before you listen to me–doctor knows best. I just want you to be able to do this in a different way than you've ever done it before.

Like I said in the disclaimer, I'm not a doctor or personal trainer, but I am someone who has been there and turned to medicine for a quick fix. I learned from personal experience that there are some things that you just have to endure without the help of anything else.

We've started off with at least two days a week. Now build upon that, adding an extra day or two once you start getting comfortable. As your body gets stronger and you start building up endurance, you have to push yourself. If you just continue with the same comfortable routine, then your body will adjust and you won't make any progress.

You have to continually push your body to the limit to get to the next level, so push it. The keys are to keep pushing your body and to be consistent. You want to form patterns that will stay with you and help you to develop discipline that you can use in other areas of your life. If you can, workout at least four or five days a week, even if you are skinny. Work at it for a half hour to get your blood pumping and to build your endurance.

We started out with getting fit because it trains you to have discipline, it helps you learn how to build routines, and it helps you learn how to push yourself beyond what you think are your limits. Before moving on, remember and apply these guidelines we talked about in the first chapter:

1. Be consistent.
2. Reach out for support by working out with a friend.
3. Don't give up even if everything in you is screaming to do so.

You are working on this radical change for yourself, but why not help someone else to get in shape? How about getting your whole family involved in this? How about friends that you know are out of shape? Can they join you on this first part of your journey? We're making radical changes; wouldn't it be a radical concept to help other people get fit and change their bad habits, too?

Use the habits you develop from physical fitness to get mentally and emotionally fit

Just the nature of getting your body fit will help your emotional stability. You'll "feel" stronger, and that strength will carry into your feelings. Were you or are you an overly emotional person? Think about it, and be real with yourself—let's work on it together.

In order to succeed in your progress, you have to have the ability to keep your emotions in check and realize when they're trying to lead you astray. For example, if you're working out and you start to feel mad, your emotions will tell you to stop working out and go home—ignore them. If you are on a consistent workout routine, you will feel stronger, and that will push some of those old emotions away. Just realize where you stand, and realize that what you're doing is right for you, so you won't give in to those feelings.

Just as with working out, you have to start gradually when learning how to keep your emotions in check, especially if you tend to be an emotional person. Don't worry, don't get discouraged; even if you have been extremely emotional your whole life, you can change. Remember that you are the one who holds the power to change—so do it!

When a situation arises that gets you all hot and bothered, walk away, take a deep breath, and think it through. The temptation is to act quickly and rashly, but remember that we are making radical changes. You need to get fit both physically and emotionally.

Be the master of your emotions; don't let them be your master!

Getting mentally fit is based on the same principles as getting physically fit; the key is to keep your mind engaged. This is going to mean some changes that you might think are radical. You're going to have to unplug all the electronic stuff.

Turn that TV off, stop going to those movies, stop being on your phone so much. I'm not telling you to do this forever (calm down!) but just long enough to get your mind fit; only a fit mind can lead you through your other changes. If you are going to succeed at radically changing your life, your mind has to be at the top of its game, ready to handle anything.

A lot of very successful people say they have time for the numerous things they have to do because they have cut out TV. I'm not telling you that this is a requirement for radical change, unless TV is a distraction for you. Always ask yourself if what you're doing is taking away time from something that could better benefit your life.

When was the last time you read a good book? Can't remember? THAT'S A PROBLEM!

There are a lot of things that are free these days and not all of them are good. Some of these "free" things will drain you of your time and your mind (TV), and many are designed to sell something to you, to take your money. Don't fall for any of these traps (that's a goal this year, right?). Take advantage of the best free resource out there (okay, second best, water is first): READING.

Want to hear a little secret? There are entire libraries full of free books that hold enough information on any subject you can think of to make you a genius. In these days of TV and the Internet, we have completely forgotten about reading–it's a lost art. I hope not for you. If you haven't been a reader in the past, why not start?

In this economy, companies are looking for the person who stands out from everyone else, and reading can help with that. Think about this: You're in an interview talking about different things; how impressed would the interviewer be if you were knowledgeable about whatever subject interested him or her?

Want to learn a new language? Read about it.

Want to learn about a specific company and what they do? Read about it.

Want to learn about setting up a website for a new business? Read about it.

All these things can help you get a better job, move ahead in your current job, or start a new business. I think you get what I'm talking about. Take advantage of the beautiful words, stories, and knowledge that are in books. When I'm traveling, and sometimes when I'm working, I like to listen to a good fiction audiobook; for the most part, I enjoy nonfiction that can teach me things. With all the books available, you have many choices, so enjoy what's available!

In addition to this direct help, reading certain books or articles will give you tools to develop mental fitness. Reading not only teaches you, it also helps you develop mental discipline by sitting there and completing books. There's no limit to how reading can help you with wisdom and mental strength, so pick up a good book and make it a part of getting mentally fit.

Besides reading, there are a lot of other ways to get mentally fit; you could probably write me a whole page of suggestions. How about playing some checkers or chess with a friend or your kids? The key is to keep that mind moving with things that won't drag it down.

Make it a family thing: Why not have family game nights? How excited would your kids be about this? I know that at first your kids are going to scream about not being able to play their videogames, but kids get over stuff like that. If you make this a family thing where you're spending time with them, and they are not off by themselves, they will love it and adapt to it.

Think about what this will do for them in the future. You will be ahead of 90 percent of the other parents out there by turning the videogames off and getting your kids mentally fit. Even if you don't care enough to do this for yourself, do it for your kids and your family. As a side benefit, your spouse or partner will be super-loving seeing what positive changes you're trying to make for your family—trust me! This is how you help yourself get mentally fit; this is how you start to radically change your life.

The end of the second step

So we are here at the end of the second step and it's time for a little review:

We have identified the things we truly want to change, and started to take action on them gradually. These are things that others would think are radical, but we are tired of the same-old same-old!

We have reached out to talk to some people that will be our support group, who will help us get through the tough times; they are there and ready to help.

We are on a regular workout routine and pushing ourselves harder every day.

We have worked out some of the emotional issues that have made us stumble in the past, and are not reacting rashly or overemotionally.

We have strengthened our mind by turning off the electronic distractions. We have started to read more, started to play chess or other things that have strengthened our mind. We can even listen to great, stimulating podcasts that give us ideas to help this process!

So how's it going? Need to vent or yell at me? As I mentioned, you can find me at kimanziconstable.com. This is also where you can share the victories or struggles you have encountered on your journey. The Tales of Work community is there to be a help to you!

At the end of the second step, take a minute to sit down and do a little post-game replay. Find out where you can make some improvements and where you had the greatest success. Make any adjustments that you deem necessary, and then pat yourself on the back! For some, this might be the most change you have ever made in your life. Just remember, don't get complacent, it's a marathon.

I hope you don't get overwhelmed or discouraged and just give up; we need you to do this, for yourself and for your family and friends. We still have a long way to go but we should feel good for what we have done. This is it. Our lives will never be the same after this! How does it feel?

You're working out now, you have more energy, and you are reading and learning.

You're doing well: KEEP UP THE GOOD WORK!

Chapter 3:

Chapter 3:

Getting Rid
of the Negative
(Third Step)

As our second step, we got our minds and our bodies fit, which will help us out tremendously as we embark on the next part of our journey. Each step in the change process helps us to move forward systematically. If you look at it this way and keep on working at it, you'll see change like you've never seen it before in your life.

We'll move forward one more step by getting rid of anything or anyone that is negative in our life. Negative people or situations can cripple our progress towards change and can derail us from our dreams. I told you up front that this book is about radical change, and that might mean cutting ties with that best friend that you've had for the last ten years! It might mean you have to give up your favorite restaurant. Change requires sacrifice, remember?

Negative eating habits

Since our last step we talked about getting fit, I thought it would be a natural progression to add the element of cleaning up any negative eating habits. How is your diet? What kinds of things do you REALLY like to eat? Remember, to get the most out of this book and to effect real change, you have to be brutally honest with yourself! It's not wrong to like things that aren't healthy for you; I have a terrible sweet tooth myself. You can like all the bad stuff you want, as long as you exercise some self-control.

Investigating your food

First, take a mental inventory or even write it down on paper. Some of you might already know which things you eat that you need to cut out of your life. We want to cut out the "junk," which for each of us might be defined somewhat differently; it has to be a personal decision. Watch the things that you are eating, see what you'd like to change, and get going.

Why does it matter?

You have seen the data; you've probably read even more articles than I on eating the right way. We know about the harm that processed foods do to our bodies. Let's look at it from more of a personal perspective: doesn't eating junk food weigh you down, make you drag all day? You might drink a soda, eat a candy bar, and get a quick burst of energy, but what happens after a few hours? That's right, it wears off, and you feel like taking a long nap.

What about all that work we did to get our bodies fit? What do you think will happen if you continue to eat junk food? All that progress you made will evaporate! As a practical matter, change those negative eating habits to keep this process moving forward.

I won't be super-specific and get into things like going vegan or not eating red meat. Those are personal choices that you have to make; you know what you need to get into your body to keep things operating on the highest level.

When I lost 132 pounds a few years ago, the one lesson I really learned was moderation. You can eat some of the things you like, you just have to eat a lot less of them. You can do it!

Purging negative people

This will be the hardest part of this journey to radically change our lives. I want to start by telling you that I've personally gone through it, so I know what I'm talking about.

I had a best friend growing up who was as close as a brother. As we grew up, we enjoyed the same things, but at one point I saw that I wasn't happy with the direction my life was going in. I told my friend about it, and mentioned some of the things I wanted to change. I thought he was with me; I was wrong. To make a long story short, he wanted to do the things we did when we were younger, he didn't want to grow up, and I did. To this day, he still acts like he's eighteen years old, with no progress on any of the things we talked about doing when we got older.

Is there someone like this in your life right now?

People that aren't on the same page will hold you back

Are you friends right now with someone who is negative? With every move you try to make, everything you talk about doing, does that person respond in a negative way? Perhaps they shoot you down; they might even make fun of you. They try to stop you with peer pressure (at any age), they do anything to keep you at the same level they are unable to escape. These are the people you have to let go, if you want to see radical change in your life.

Look, it's going to be hard enough to hit the gym, cut out junk food, and do the other things you have to do. It will be ten times worse if you have someone always in your ear telling you how stupid it is to do what you are doing. You don't need that stress!

Radical change requires that you not let anyone or anything keep you from changing your life. I don't care how long you've been close to someone, if they stand in your way or try and stop your progress, they have got to go.

Who has to go?

As you are reading this, can you think of any people in your life who are like this? How long have you been friends? It's really going to suck, but they might have to go. You want to give those people the benefit of the doubt, so go to them, tell them that you want to radically change your life, and tell them why. If they are truly your friend they will respect your decision; they might even change their attitude. It would be great to have one more cheerleader on your side.

If they still laugh at you or won't support you, you're going to have to cut ties, maybe not forever but until they can respect you and what you're doing. You don't need anything negative in your life; negativity will keep you where you are now or even drag you farther from where you want to be.

Getting rid of negative distractions

We have talked about the big two: food and people. If you can get rid of all the negatives in those areas then getting rid of your other negative distractions should be a piece of cake (just kidding). The process is the same: you have to be the one to determine what your negative distractions are, but anything that takes away from moving forward to a better life has to go.

Could TV watching be a negative distraction? How much TV do you watch? Is there anything else you could be doing with that time? You have to examine whether you have enough time to work on your dreams and also watch your favorite shows. For me the answer is no. "So what are you saying, cut out TV?" Maybe so; I can't see how it will help you further your dreams.

What about videogames and other electronic things? Could you be working out, but instead you have to play the latest video or pc game? You're reading this book and have gotten this far for a reason, and I firmly believe that reason is strong enough to keep you from being distracted by the little nonsense things of life!

How about time spent on social media? You may need it to promote your work, I get that. Do you get wrapped up in all the little games on some of these sites? Do you get caught up in reading everyone's updates and commenting on them?

I'm not saying ignore the things that are important in your life

Don't misunderstand what I'm saying to you right now, I'm not telling you to ignore your spouse or kids and tell them that I said they were distractions (I don't want that hate mail!). Everything has to be in its proper time and place; put first things first.

You're going to hit a little bit of a wall with some of these changes. You're going to have to figure out what the proper balance is. Keep the important things of life first: family, spouse, maybe some work, you know what's important. That's why you might have to cut out things like TV so that you can use that time for changing your life.

How will your family or friends react if you cut out distractions to make radical change in your life?

Work into it slowly

I realize how hard this step will be, especially if you have to cut ties with a friend or friends that you have had all your life. The best way to make any change is to do it gradually, take it slow. This is a nine-step plan on purpose; you might think that devoting a whole chapter to getting rid of negative distractions is too much, but it's not. You may need a whole month for this step, taking it week by week and cutting out all that is negative. Maybe you should work on a different aspect each week.

The goal is to create positive habits that complement and reinforce the radical changes you're making. This will help you have the best chance of long-term success.

Falling and getting up

You are going to fall down; the key is that you have to get right back up. Suppose you fall down five times; you have to learn how to get up five times. There's a temptation to just give up when we fall down–it's human nature. I say, fight that part of human nature with everything you've got.

You'll get many victories and then you'll fail. Get back up. No one is perfect, no one will stay on their feet 100 percent of the time. We are all trying to do the same things here; we're trying to radically change our lives.

Sometimes you might get tired of this journey; you might even be tired just reading this. Go eat some refreshing fruit, get a little energy, and get back on track. Remember how we established our support group? Call them and get some encouragement.

We're at the end of the third step, and you're doing great. Hopefully you've made more progress than you've ever made before, so keep it up! As always, take a little time at the end of each step to reflect on where you've been and where you're going.

Smile to yourself; you do remember that we're supposed to be savoring the journey, right?

SAVOR IT!

Chapter 4:

Chapter 4:

Fixing

Your Money

(Fourth Step)

How's it going so far, are you with me? I hope as you're reading this, you have started down your own personal journey. It's time for something new for all of us! Now that we're starting to take things to the next level, we're going to get "serious" because we're talking about money.

Money can be a very touchy subject for most of us, but since we're talking about radical change, we have to talk about it!

Money is the gas in our radical change gas tank

As you proceed through this book, you'll see me talking about different things that can't be done without some money.

Even if you decide that I'm a hack and you don't want to do any of what I've laid out, you should at least read this chapter on money. I believe it can help other areas of your life whether or not you decide on the radical change I propose.

Look back at chapter one, where you mapped out some of the things that you wanted to change. On the list you made, how many of the items will require money? If you are light on funds or aren't where you want to be financially, what can you do? (Don't go out and rob a bank!)

At this point in your journey it's time to get really serious about money, both how you spend it and how you save it.

Are you living paycheck to paycheck?

I'm going to let you in on a little secret about my past. Back in the day, I was able to do a little magic! All right, let me be honest, it wasn't exactly magic; I'm talking about writing magical checks that "floated." What?

Don't act like you don't know what I'm talking about. "Floating" a check was when you didn't have enough money in your account to cover it, but a bill was overdue, so you sent the check out anyway–hoping you would be able to deposit your paycheck before it came in for processing. Like I said, magic (Ha!). For me those days are over, and I hope you either have never done this or are in a financial position where you don't have to do it anymore!

The reason I had to do this was because I was living paycheck to paycheck.

I had no savings, and even the smallest unexpected circumstance threatened to ruin my life! I don't think I need to tell you that this is no way to live; you must have a little cushion for all those unexpected things life will throw at you. So be honest with me (and yourself), how much money do you have saved in case of an emergency? If something happened now—car repairs, broken water heater, or any other kind of mini-disaster—how would you get through it?

You need an emergency fund

Many people and families have fallen apart over shoddy finances. You have to have a backup plan to fall back on. Here are a few thoughts that hopefully will be a help in this regard:

You need an emergency fund! I've hit on this already, just a little, but let's get specific. The experts will tell you to have at least three to six months' worth of your expenses, if you can do this, great! For me (and maybe you), this wasn't a realistic possibility right away. So I took Dave Ramsey's suggestion and set aside $1,000 as a small, starter emergency fund. Three to six months would be great, but my financial situation was not healthy enough to hit that right away. I liked the idea of $1,000 because it was attainable and it would cover 90 percent of the emergencies that might come up. Maybe you can't get $1,000 right away, so start with $100—work your way up to $1,000, a week at a time, and you'll get there eventually.

Cut out excess spending: Do you have to have those three sodas every day at work? Do you have to get fast food for lunch? Do you really need a bigger TV just because it's on sale? You know there's junk you can cut out of your life right now so you could start an emergency fund, right?

CUT OUT ALL THAT UNNECESSARY STUFF FROM YOUR LIFE!

Pick up extra work: If you're having trouble saving up a little extra cash, why not pick up some overtime or some odd jobs? There's a wealth of untouched opportunity because people think certain things are beneath them. How about cutting grass, shoveling snow, cleaning houses, or any other kind of odd job to make some cash? Most people think they are doing just fine and they won't do these minimum-wage jobs. You can take them and use the money to build up your emergency fund!

Make saving and planning a way of life: I'm sure even before you read this chapter you knew that living paycheck to paycheck was stupid. This isn't new information. So the question is, "Why don't you have an emergency fund already?" Whenever you want to accomplish lasting change with anything in life, the best way to do it is to make it a habit–quick fixes don't work. Changing your financial situation can't be about saving a couple hundred bucks and then going back to the same old lifestyle–it won't last. You have to form a habit of saving money, watching how you spend your hard-earned money, and thinking about your financial future.

Take it one step at a time: The best way to do any of this is to take it step by step. Cut out that soda, and put away the money you would have spent on it in a jar somewhere. The end result will be that you develop good habits that also affect other areas of your life. If you skip drinking that soda, you'll lose a little weight; once you lose the weight, you'll be more active with family and friends... You see how it works. Come on, you know I'm right, give it a try!

Take the first steps forward

The key to generating an emergency fund and creating habits that will change your life is to take the first step. So when you get your paycheck this week, set aside a little money for your emergency fund; it could change your life forever. Remember, once you make a little progress, you can't stop and be happy with just making progress. Don't get complacent. Move forward towards your goal and don't stop until you've changed your life and no longer fear the unexpected. The best way to combat the unexpected is having and sticking to a well thought-out plan.

So do you have a plan? Do you have money set aside? If not, I hope today is the day you start saving money for whatever emergencies life will throw at you during this journey of change. You have seen that money is your foundation. You need an emergency fund, but you will also need a change fund.

The change fund

I've mentioned several times that our family is moving to Hawaii. We have set up a "change fund" to help make that happen. Our plan is to have at least $15,000 in that fund by the end of this year.

The change fund is money that will fill any void, such as loss of income while we transition; it's money that we will live on. For you, the needs might be a little different–you might need that money for some other aspect of your change plans.

The point is that for some of the bigger things you may have set as your goals (starting a business, moving somewhere else, donating to charity, for a few examples), you're going to need to set up some kind of a fund and you will have to start contributing regularly to that fund!

In order to do these two steps, the emergency fund and the change fund, you'll either have to get a better, higher-paying job or look at where you're spending your money and cut out the waste!

Watching your spending

You're pretty smart, so I don't need to tell you that every single cent of your money counts!

Last year I had a work schedule where I wasn't getting much sleep, so to stay awake I would get a Mountain Dew from the gas station from time to time. This started out as a way to keep me up but quickly moved into a bad habit that I indulged even when I wasn't working. As you probably already know, Mountain Dew can be addictive. I would buy a 44-ounce soda every day at the cost of 83 cents. That's not much money, right?

There probably are little things you spend money on every day without even a second thought; they cost the same amount of money that you might find in your couch cushions. You can see where I'm going with this. All those "little things" add up to a good amount of money in the end, money you could use for a number of different goals and dreams.

Do you have an emergency fund set up? Could you create one, if you cut out those frivolous little expenses?

I know it can be hard sometimes at work when you get hungry; you just want a little snack from the vending machine and you have two bucks in your pocket. As hard as it is, you could greatly benefit if you resist the temptation. If you're self-employed like me, the temptation comes in the way of buying fast food. It's so much easier to just pull in the drive-thru at McDonald's and buy a quick lunch, and you don't even need cash anymore.

The Problem

If your goal is to get out of a job you don't love, or to move on to something or somewhere you've been dreaming about, then be aware that every single candy bar or trip to a fast food place delays that dream. Think about what 83 cents per day for Mountain Dew adds up to in a year: $302.95. How much does fast food add up to, even if you only go one or two times a week? In order to move forward, you're going to need money to make it work; in order to be more secure, you're going to need some money as an emergency fund. That $302.95 could be the start of my emergency fund. How will you start yours?

How can you put a stop to it?

Remember back in the day, when your mom used to pack you a bag lunch for school? As you already know, you can pack a lunch for work; you can put more than just lunch in that bag, have a whole bunch of little snacks in there. I really didn't need that soda every day to keep me up. Buying some healthy oranges gave me the boost I needed at a much cheaper price.

You have to realize that it's all connected

If you cut out fast food, sodas, that candy bar, or whatever little thing you're into, what do you think the results would be? You would have more money in your pocket, and you would also eliminate the junk from your eating habits. You might then lose a little weight and feel a lot better. I felt like I needed that soda, but after a month of not drinking it, it seemed as if I had as much energy as my kids. You see how one area affects another?

A small challenge for you

Actions speak louder than words, so why not test out my theory. For the next month, try not to spend money on even the smallest items at work or even in your home life. See if you end up with more money, and check the scales to see if it helps your weight. If I'm wrong, you'll have more money to spend when you go back to buying junk. Can you try this for just one month?

I hope you decide to take me up on this challenge. I think if we band together and try this, we can serve as each other's support system. You're here reading this book, probably because you're pursuing your dreams and trying to move on to work that you would love. Cutting out the little stuff and saving that money will help you get closer to those dreams!

This step we are working on our money, how we spend it and how we can actually save it. We have seen that we're going to need money later on down the line, to help with some of the bigger changes we want to make.

Just as we had to get physically fit, we have to get financially fit; this journey is all about radical change. Some of you may be reading this and think I'm radical; that's good. That means the message is coming across!

When you've completed this step, take some time just as I always suggest: sit down quietly and reflect on where you were, where you are, and what you've been able to accomplish so far. It will amaze you. Look at the areas of success and the areas of failure, fix what needs to be fixed, and copy what's working for you.

Don't forget to just sit back and enjoy the ride!

Chapter 5:

Chapter 5:

Nail Down Your Plans (Fifth Step)

Now that we have gotten some basic things out of the way, it's time to get a little more serious. We need to write down our plans and start implementing changes to make these plans happen.

What do you mean?

Let me give you an example from my life: We first started taking about retiring in Hawaii after a few years, when the kids would have left the house and we were older. Through a series of events, we changed our thought process and decided to move next year (scary!). When we made this decision, we had a general idea of what we wanted to do. We did the first step from this book: we sat down and identified what we wanted.

Both my wife and I are overweight, and we knew that as part of all our changes we wanted to get fit, so since the beginning of this year we have been going to the YMCA as a family. As we told family and friends about our plans to move, some were supportive, but most thought we were nuts. There were a few who "crossed the line" into the negative category, and we asked them to just respect our decision for our family. They didn't. So, since we had to take the step of cutting anything negative out of our life, they had to go. These were the second and third steps I've described in the book.

Next we started writing things out so we could see the big picture. For my family this consists of how we are going to pay our bills, where we're going to live, where our kids are going to go to school, and how much money we'll need for all of this.

Since money is the foundation for making radical change possible, I made it the fourth step in the plan. For our fifth step we will nail down the details of how that money will be spent. This is the sort of work I'm talking about in this chapter. Now let me describe things a little more clearly.

Write down the "big" steps in the plan

The best way to conquer huge steps and make radical plans is to see the whole picture clearly, right in front of your face. Write your plan down somewhere; whether it's on paper or on your iPad, write down the main points of the plan.

Going back to the example of me and my family, we wrote down things like, "find an area to live." Later we added sub points such as locating schools and managing living costs, as we went along.

This step requires you to do some hardcore thinking and really get serious about what you want to change in your life. I know that you're already serious, but it's time for details; this part requires extra determination. So is your brain buzzing right now? That's a good thing, roll with it; if you have to, put this book down and get to work (make sure you come back though). You don't want to cut off those creative juices!

Don't think you have to know it all right away. The title of this chapter is *Nail down your plans*, but the point of this step's work is that you start with a general idea but by the end of the step you get more focused and more specific.

You're not going to feel like it

I have to let you in on some news: You're never going to feel like doing what you know you not only should, but also need to do!

There have been at least a million times when I've set a goal to do something that I knew was right and good for our future plans, but when the time came, I didn't feel like doing it anymore.

Has this ever happened to you?

The thing to remember about fulfilling our goals and dreams is that we can't rely on our feelings; they will betray us every time. If you struggle with this, a little or a lot, here are three guidelines to help you get past your feelings:

Do it anyway: If you have set a goal to lose weight this year, and the Monday comes when you plan on going to the gym–after a hard day of work you might not "feel" like it. When you have that gym bag in your hand, and that voice in your head says "you had a hard day of work, you'll go tomorrow," you need to tell that voice to shut up, get your car keys and go to the gym. You may not feel like it, but I guarantee that, after working out, you'll feel better and be glad you went. Remember to make this a habit in your life!

Have a friend help you out: In this same scenario, what if you had the gym trip planned out with a friend, or you called a friend when you began to have second thoughts? If it's a real friend, I'm sure they'll help out; they'll encourage you to go to the gym. Even as adults we still have a little fear of peer pressure; use this to push you past "not feeling like it." We devoted a whole section to setting up a support group. This is what it's for! When you don't "feel" like it, call on some people from your group.

Make it a habit: I've talked about this in detail in blog posts. If you form a habit to help with certain goals in your life, your feelings won't even be able to dream of stopping you. If you form a habit of working out four days a week, and keep it up for six months straight, then whenever the feeling of not wanting to do it creeps in, it will fade out quickly. Program your body and mind to do the work. The habit will win in the end!

I have talked about this in the context of working out, but "not feeling like" doing something can apply to anything in your life, to any changes you're making, and the same principles apply. If it was up to our feelings we would never go anywhere. We would stay home, sleep for ten hours a day, and spend the rest of the day watching TV and eating. We don't need these feelings; we need habits. We need to resolve to accomplish all our goals and dreams and changes.

Remember, if you set your mind to it, form habits, and have determination, you can make this the most fruitful year of your life. This goes hand in hand with *living, not just existing*. Ignoring those feelings and knocking out your goals is truly living!

Don't be a spectator to your life because your "feelings" have sidetracked you–LIVE YOUR LIFE!

As you progress, get more specific

You have to be constantly thinking and scheming about the big changes you have planned; then as your plans become more solid in your mind, start writing them down. You started by writing down the main points of what you want to do; about halfway through this step, fill in the sub points.

We are already in the fifth step of our nine-step plan, and we have a lot left to do. We need to get some sub points filled in so we know what to do next.

Remember, it doesn't have to be perfect, but you should be progressing on your plan.

Don't panic or feel pressured

I don't know about you, but when I work under pressure I make mistakes; so don't get panicked. Yeah, you're in the fifth step, but you're making radical changes that will affect your whole life. You want to be sure. If you are trying to nail down plans, but all you can see when you look at your paper is a bunch of lines, don't worry. That just means you have to go back, rethink your plan a little bit more, no need to get a nosebleed (lol).

Feeling too tired

Do you remember the excitement you had the first time you discovered what your dreams are, the first time you started working on them? Do you remember what it was like taking the first step of this journey? Do you remember the excitement, the thrill of it all? Is it fading a little?

It seemed like no matter what happened, nothing was going to stop you. You might have had a few hiccups, there might have been some naysayers, but it didn't matter because you were on the path to fulfilling your dreams! If you had a busy schedule during the day, you would stay up into the wee hours of the morning because you were fulfilling your dreams. If you had to buy some equipment, you didn't mind working overtime or whatever it took. I know exactly how you felt because this is also how I have felt.

Having said that, here's the question: Do you still have that drive and ambition, or when you think about doing extra work to accomplish your dreams do you want to just roll over and take a nap?

If this describes you (as it did me), I want to give you a little encouragement to help you get over the "hump." Here are three things that will help you push through this bump in the road to fulfilling your radical changes:

Take a nap! Maybe the reason thinking about doing extra work makes you tired is that you are literally tired. Makes sense right? What about those workouts from getting fit? Maybe you already work a full-time job, and you come home worn out. You might have been able to ignore it in the excitement of the first stages of your path, but in the end you are human.

Being human, you need an adequate amount of rest. Only you know how much rest you need every day. Make sure you distinguish between exhaustion and just being lazy (if you slept ten hours and are too tired to get something done, then maybe you're just being lazy!), but if you're tired, sleep! You may think you're going to get more accomplished by pushing through the sleepiness, but I think you would find that you were actually less productive and your work might be a little sloppier because of being tired. Get some rest.

Do something every day: You might get tired just reading this sentence, but this is important. Have you ever heard of momentum? Even if you have just ten minutes a day, it's still better than nothing. I know you can make more than ten minutes a day for your dream! When you take a day away, it will eventually turn into two, then two will turn into four, and before you know it three weeks will have passed and you won't even remember what your dream was. Keep it fresh in your mind by constantly working on it; give yourself some momentum by making progress every day. It will be awesome and inspiring to see how much progress you can make by chipping away at it a little at a time! This is a nine-step plan; don't overdo the pressure, but a little pressure won't kill you! This plan requires you to work on it every day, so that you can move on to the next step.

Focus on the "why" of what you're doing: A lot of times it's human nature to look at the details of something and get overwhelmed, frustrated, angry, and eventually just give up (this is the easy way out). The major point is that when you focus on the reason why you're doing something, it makes all the frustrating parts more bearable. For example, when I thought about writing this second book, I'd get to the computer after having a long day at my job. I'd feel too tired to work, and mad that I hadn't been able to make the transition faster. I'd look at my book sales, and be happy but not excited; there weren't 10,000 copies sold the night before. I very easily talked myself out of writing any of the second book that day.

Lately I have looked at why I need to write this second book (more time home with my family, doing something that I love every day, being able to help others that are struggling). That gives me a shot of energy to press on and keep going hard! If you are getting overwhelmed, if you are tired of looking at the "how" and the "what," stop and focus on "why" you're doing what you're doing!

Why do you want to make these radical changes in your life? By now you should know the reason and be able to focus on it, and that's what will help get you through any feelings of being tired.

It's very easy to justify not working on our dreams; after all, we have day jobs that take up a tremendous amount of time out of our week. We are working on a lot of different things right now in this effort to make big, radical changes.

Ask yourself this, though—what's the alternative? If you can't find that energy, can't make time to work on your dreams and changes, then you had better make plans to keep doing something you hate until you snap or they fire you! The alternative is to stay in the same lifestyle that you have already acknowledged you're not happy with.

Scary, isn't it? Don't give up, don't be discouraged. Take a nap right now, and wake up determined that you're going to do what it takes to get to your dreams. I know you have it in you!

By the end of this step you should have your blueprint

As you reach the end of this fifth step you should have the basic blueprint for whatever changes you're making. You started by writing down the main points; as you thought more about it you filled in some of the sub-points. For example, if you're moving somewhere new, you should have written down a rough estimate of the cost of moving; you should have defined the general area where you want to live. If you want to run a marathon, you should have the date of your first marathon and know its route.

The point is to make progress as you work on each step and to build upon that progress.

We're at the end of the fifth step, it's time for a checkup.

How are you doing?

Are you still working out?

How's your diet?

Are there any negative people in your life?

Have you cut out excess spending and started saving for your future plans?

Do you have the basic blueprint you'll use for making radical change?

We're going into the sixth step and we'll be starting to move forward with our plans; if you're behind, just catch up. Take a deep breath, relax. This is the rest of your life.

We're going to enjoy this process, remember? Enjoy it, and keep moving forward.

Chapter 6:

Chapter 6:

Make the

First Moves

(Sixth Step)

We've done some planning; we have established a basic blueprint for radical change. Now it's time for some "real" steps. It's time to move forward with these changes.

Are you moving somewhere new?

As you know, we are planning on moving to Hawaii next year. Are you moving to a new place, a new state, or a new country? If you are, then this step will be the time to do a little more in-depth, on-location research. At some point, even if it's just for a weekend, go to the new place and see if it's everything you think it will be. You can do a lot of research online and that's a great way to explore, but there's no substitute for actually being there, seeing and feeling the atmosphere.

Now if you're moving to India or Africa, a weekend trip might not be realistic; but if it's at all possible, try and take a trip. If you can take your family or a close friend, that will help. Really the planning for this trip should have been part of the fifth step; if you're reading the whole book first, start planning a survey trip as soon as possible.

What to do on your survey trip

Let's assume you were able to work it out so you can go on a survey trip; what should you do while you're there? Now, this will all be common sense stuff, so bear with me.

On your trip, try to see your new place from the eyes of a resident, not a tourist. There's a danger of going on a trip and getting caught up in the joy of not working; each day, you tell yourself that you'll start looking into everything tomorrow. The days keep going by, you haven't learned anything new, you come home–what are you going to do now, lie to your spouse? You don't want that do you?

Get to your new place and hit the ground running; on day one you should already know where you're going to visit and what you have to accomplish each day. Better than that, you should have your exact itinerary set up ahead of time; this will keep you from wasting time. Have you figured out where you want to live in the new place? Go there. Talk to some people who are living there, ask them for the negatives, and try to digest the information.

Look at the basics of life while you're there. If you have kids, where are the good schools? Look at stores: where are you going to buy your food? If you're going to some place exotic, like Hawaii, it's especially important to see where the grocery stores are.

You're smart, so I won't go into everything that you should look for, but the point is to be serious. You're making a radical change, possibly moving to a radically different place; you've got some serious work to do.

Use your survey trip in planning

Take the knowledge you gain from this trip and use it in planning the "big" move. You now have a better, more realistic idea of what things are like in the area where you're thinking of moving. You have an idea of how much things cost. You have valuable information that can help confirm your decision or make you rethink your plan.

I'm going with the premise that you're sure about your move, and that this survey trip just solidified that decision. Take the information you gained and adjust your budget; maybe you need to be saving more, maybe less (save more anyway!), but plug in this information and get to work.

With proper planning and hard work, we both can move to the places of our dreams!

Do you want to change jobs?

If one of the big things you want to change is your job, then the first step is to identify what you want to do. My first book was all about this. Many people just look for whatever job is open or pays well and apply to that job—but not us. We're making radical change, so this new job has to be the job of our dreams. To best find your dream job, you have to figure out some things about yourself; what do you like in a job, and what do you hate? Is there something that you've been dreaming about since you were a little kid? That dream job, that one job that you think about and feel happy, that's what we're looking for.

This chapter is about taking first steps; however, if you see an opportunity to get the job, go for it!

Like I said before, most people just want a job that pays well, but that's the wrong move! Every day people are in jobs they hate, so they take to the Internet, they look in the classifieds, etc. That just won't work, and it's absolutely contrary to our plan for radical change.

Can I make this point any clearer? This model might have worked back in the day, but with the current state of our economy and the lack of jobs, this won't work anymore!

Think about this: when a company advertises that they are hiring, how many people do you think will apply? Companies will receive thousands of applications for posted jobs. So when a company advertises for a job, it's already too late for you! WHAT? Trust me.

Here's a tip for you: Sit down and think long and hard about where you want to work and what you want to do for work. Once you've figured that out, get a list of ten companies that fit into those criteria. Whether or not (hopefully not) they are advertising in any way, they are hiring. Apply at those companies. That's the tip: apply when you have less competition!

With this economy you'll always have competition trying to get a job. Applying at companies that don't seem to be hiring will dramatically increase your odds of getting a good job. If you're a good fit for that company, whether they're officially hiring or not, they'll find a way to get you in.

This should be a job that you'll love and maybe do for a long time, although with us "living" our lives we may be moving around. The key is to make sure to pick what's right for you!

How about starting a business?

You read all the stories in the news about how bad things are, and they seem to only get worse. You hear about big companies filing for bankruptcy and many going out of business... it's scary, right?

So, how could you start a business in this situation with this economy?

I hope that, having read the book this far, you believe anything is possible. It's not about making some changes one day and then it's over; it's about proper planning and hard work. You can use the same principles to start your dream business and actually have tremendous success. The only thing that can stand in the way of your success is yourself–do you truly believe it?

You are all about radical change, and if starting a business is a part of that, then nothing will stop you. The reason you'll survive where others have failed? You'll work harder at it, separating yourself from any competition. They're just trying to make money; you're changing your life and truly living!

So, it's time take the first actions to start your business. What will you need to open it? How much will everything cost? What (if any) kind of equipment will you need? Will you need to obtain permits and licenses? Find out. Do the research to determine exactly what you'll need to move forward with your plan. Take the first actions.

Start operating on a small scale; for example, if you want to open a restaurant, start a small catering business. If you want to write books, start some blogs and write away. The key to this step is to end up with something to show for your work, some sort of tangible progress.

It applies to a lot of different things

I've listed the top two things that people will want to change in their lives, but the technique applies to anything you want to change.

Here's a warning, though: As you make these first steps, watch out for a silent enemy–doubt!

Even though you are doing something that you know is right and that you should be doing, you're still going to have doubt.

Tell me if this sounds familiar: you've made a certain decision in your life, like moving somewhere else, getting a new job, or starting a business. You're all pumped and ready to take the world by storm. Then one day you're doing something and BOOM: you hear that little voice in your head saying things like: "You can't afford to move," "They're never going to hire you," "That business won't work in this economy." Has this happened to you? I bet it has–that's doubt!

Suppose you're planning that new venture, and a friend who finds out says it's a bad idea; maybe even a family member says that? No matter what you do or how well you plan for things, you'll always have doubts! It's natural and a part of human nature.

So you pretty much have two choices: give in to the doubt, and give up, or press ahead with what you know you should be doing, and keep on making the radical changes to make your plan work. Which will you choose?

Here are three tools to help you fight doubt:

Proper planning: You're smart enough to know that without a proper plan you won't accomplish anything, and doubt will win with little or no fight. Use a plan. When you plan, be specific as to what you want to accomplish and what time frame you will allow for each step. You might still have doubts, but executing a proper plan will make those doubts look silly. Since you have been using a proper plan this whole time, you need to trust that plan. You don't have to doubt, you've got this!

Don't listen to people who are negative: You know you have those friends in your life who are always quick to shoot down your ideas. When you have doubt in the back of your mind about something, avoid those people! If you have been following this plan, then those people should already be gone; if for some reason you allowed them back, then tell them they better shape up or take a hike. People will always be negative, especially if things aren't going right in their own lives, so don't listen to them! You're an adult, and you can make your own decisions without the influence of others, so do it!

Take action: The best way to combat doubt is to ignore it and take action! You know what you should do, so why hesitate? Go for it! Life is too short to be sidelined by doubt; if you listen to those voices you'll never accomplish anything, and you'll die after a miserable life. Is that what you're looking for? Haven't you come too far to struggle with these day-one issues?

You have big goals and big plans to make radical change. You can be sure doubt will creep in. I've given you a few tools to fight it, but the choice is yours.

Will you give up or push ahead? I hope you choose to push ahead!

We're here at the end of the sixth step, and we're starting to move past the "prep work" and into taking action. We're making gradual changes, but also taking advantage of any opportunities that are coming our way. I hope you're following through and not giving up.

Relax. Smile. You're closer than you think to radically changing your life!

Chapter 7:

Chapter 7:

Tying Up

Loose Ends

(Seventh Step)

We are getting close to accomplishing our dreams, our goals, our plans, and radically changing our life. This chapter, we talk about closing things out in style, making sure not to burn any bridges on the way to our dreams. I'll share a few practical tips to get one step closer.

Have a backup plan

Just because you have to use plan B doesn't mean you failed at plan A!

I've been on the path to my ultimate dream job now for several months, and I have to say, I was a little naive in my expectations. I was angry at myself for a little while when I realized that it wasn't going to be as easy as I thought. I quickly got over it. It's okay to have big dreams and to shoot for the stars; that is what we should be doing. That's what this whole journey of radical change is all about, that's what this whole book is about.

Because of some new and different circumstances at my day job, I came to realize that I didn't have a plan B (it totally freaked me out!). So that's what I want to talk to you about. I just want to ask you a few questions, and hopefully I can give you a few helpful pointers.

Do you have a Plan B? I'm going to drop some serious, never before heard, ancient, amazing knowledge on you (not really): Life doesn't always work out as we planned. What? Yep, there are going to be "bumps on the road." That's what plan B is for.

I know you're amazed by how wise I am right now—not! What's your plan B, just in case your exit strategy doesn't work out? Here's a better question: what's your plan B if you lose your day job?

WHAT?

Remember, life takes unexpected turns. With the state of our economy, there's no such thing as job security anymore, and you could quite conceivably lose your day job at any time. If you don't have a plan B, even for your current job, then you could be up a tree.

How realistic is your plan B?

You may have come up with a backup plan five years ago; is it still relevant today? I remember when I had a vacation relief business, and I did really well with it, people started to take notice and plan. I would talk to other bread delivery guys from bigger companies, and they would tell me that if they lost their job they had a plan B: to set up the same business as me–my business was their back up plan. At the time I was highly irritated, thinking it was an attack on my business. As I matured I realized it was a joke; those guys wouldn't have been able to just show up and say "hire me," they would have had to put in work with a few clients first to build trust. It wouldn't have been an overnight thing.

Your plan B has to be something that will let you go out and start making money right away, not just an idea or a theory.

How quickly will you start making money with your plan B?

I got scared that I didn't have a plan B, and I started thinking of a few options. The problem was that none of these options would have yielded me money right away, and I'm not in a financial position to sustain having no income for very long! I don't know what your plan B is, but it had better yield quick money!

Those were my questions, I know there are many more, but you get the point. Let's talk about a few practical tips:

Make plans B, C, and D. I hope by now you see the wisdom in having something to fall back on; you just never know what's going to happen. So today (I'm deadly serious) start making a plan B, and after you have a solid plan B, make a C and a D.

Make sure plan B is realistic–don't be like those bread guys with false hope. Now I do believe that anything is possible, but don't think your backup plan is that you're going to be the CEO of Apple; that's not realistic! Make sure you can make some quick cash. There are a lot of things that you can do to put money in your pocket right away. They may not be the most glamorous things, but they'll pay. Can you cut grass? Can you shovel snow? Can you wash cars? Can you paint? These jobs may not be your next career, but they will put money in your pocket right away until you can fix your plan A.

I hope you will sit down seriously and come up with something to fall back on; maybe doing that will actually help point you in the direction of where you want to go in your work life. It's just smart to have something to fall back on, and it could keep you from ruin.

If for some reason you have to fall back on your plan B, don't view that as a failure. It could happen to anyone. If you are on the path to your dream job, and along the way you have to fall back onto your plan B, just view the experience as a useful lesson.

So the first loose end we tied up, as the first part of this seventh step, was to formulate a plan B to back up whatever radical changes we plan to make. If things go as planned, there is nothing to worry about and we will have some extra cash reserves. If our changes don't go as planned, which often happens in life, then we'll have something to fall back on.

If you're quitting your job, having a Plan B will help

At one point or another, each of us has thought about quitting our job, right? It's Friday, you might have just had the worst week in the world, and you can't help thinking about quitting.

You have worked hard to get to this point in your plan; you have carefully planned your journey, you took the first steps, and you now feel confident in your plans to move on to your dream job or business. Is it time?

The thing we have tried to remember throughout this book is to be smart about whatever we do, so we will also be smart about quitting our old job.

It really doesn't take much to set you off and make you want to quit, does it? It could be that annoying person you work with, or that boss who doesn't think anything you do is good enough. You could just be having one of those bad days where everything is falling over and nothing seems to be going right. Is it time to quit then?

I can't tell you when it's time to quit your job, and you'll never hear me tell you to quit, because it's a personal choice. However, if you have gotten to the point where you're confident that it really is time to quit, here are some things to help.

One more thing: having thought long and hard, are you sure your current job is not your dream job?

Don't burn any bridges on your way out

Suppose you have a solid backup plan to quit your job, and you're ready to go. Don't just quit without any notice! I know that if you have that backup plan in place, it might be tempting to finally let someone have it—but you never know what's going to happen. You might ream that boss out only to have him become your boss at your new company, six months later—how will that work out?

The world is big, but it becomes very small when it comes to people moving around in certain industries. You end up seeing the same people again. Give your two weeks' notice, and leave the right way, on good terms. It will work out better for you in the long run. Think about this: if worse comes to worst, you might want to have the option to return to that job.

Leave better than you started

You don't want to burn any bridges, and you want to reserve the right to return if you have to. The best way to make this possible is to do such incredible work on your way out that they remember you for years to come!

I know you're a good worker so you've probably been doing this all along, but when you have put in your two weeks' notice, step your work up to the next level. I'm not talking about working seventy extra hours, but each job that you do should be as close to perfect as you can make it. You know that hard assignment that nobody seems to get right? Step in and hit it out of the park. Doing this will help if you have to come back—they might even give you an offer you can't refuse until you can make things work with your dream job.

If you are going to quit your job, I hope you use these principles. They will definitely help you in the long run. Please, I repeat, please, make sure this is the right decision for yourself, and if you have a family, for them. Too many people have ruined their lives and the lives of their loved ones because of rash emotional decisions made in the heat of the moment. Don't be one of those people!

If you're moving, get rid of what you don't need

When we move to Hawaii, we plan on selling everything and only shipping one car. We want to completely simplify our lives, and that means getting rid of all the "stuff" we thought we needed. You may not be moving to an island, but could you benefit by radically changing what you have?

Prepare for your radical change by selling what you don't need. Get rid of all that stuff you don't really use anymore. You can make some much needed extra money, or perhaps donate to a charity and help someone less fortunate. You'll win by cleaning up and simplifying your life; someone else will benefit from gaining new possessions. You may not be able to get rid of everything at once, but do as much as you can.

Whatever change you're making in your life, this is the time to do the busy work, the little "cleanup tasks." If you have been following along you should have abundant new energy to tackle these things, and you should have all the right motivation.

Spend extra time with friends or loved ones

Even if you're not moving, spending this extra time will still be good for you. If you are moving out of the state or out of the country, then you absolutely need to soak up as much time as humanly possible with family and friends.

If you can spare a little extra money, then go out and do some "big" events; do things you would normally never have thought about doing. At this point you're truly living your life, enjoying every moment, and savoring the journey; take it to the next level and include your family and friends.

Mending relationships, burying the hatchet

Remember all those people you had to cut out in the beginning? What about people that you just lost touch with? It's time to reconnect. If you're leaving, then you want to get everything off your chest, to leave with a clean conscience. It's human nature for us to have bitterness, but we're radically changing our life. We can change what human nature has tried to use to trap us. We're stronger than before, we're "fit" in every way, so we can mend those relationships.

Make a list and get to it

I can't cover every scenario in this chapter, so I'm going to need your help. What are all the changes that you're making? Look at your list, look at your game plan; what do you need to tie up? Figure it out, and clean things up.

We're at the end of the seventh step. Are you excited? We're one step away from making the changes we have been dreaming of and planning for. Take some time to fine-tune things, to change any details that need to be changed.

If you need some extra time, then take it. If you're freaking out at taking the next step, then relax, and go listen to some soothing music.

Talk over any fears with your loved ones or friends, don't hold it all inside.

Are you ready?

Chapter 8:

Chapter 8:

Make Radical Changes
(Eighth Step)
THIS IS IT!

This is what it's been all about, getting to this moment and finally changing our lives forever. All of your planning, all of your dreaming has come down to this step.

It's time to radically change your life.

Don't do it unless you're ready

After having come this far in your journey, it's tempting to finish no matter what. The question is, are you truly ready for the next step?

Don't move ahead if everything is not prepared as much as possible. I know you can't completely plan for everything, but you can get pretty close. If you go forward with life-altering, radical changes when you're not ready, you run the risk of turning your dreams into nightmares and possibly ruining your life.

It's been seven steps of planning and working and extreme sacrifice. If you don't have it all together yet, it's okay to take a little more time to get things in line. Have you ever rushed a big project at work? How did that turn out? On your journey you have learned to plan, you have taken whole months with your planning; what makes you think now is the time to rush into something before you're ready?

Take the extra time if you need it. That's not failing–it's just plain smart.

Get adjusted to a new you

It's going to be kind of weird to look at yourself now compared to where you were; it's going to take a little getting used to. Don't get cocky and think you have everything figured out, because you don't. If you have moved to some new exciting place, don't be the cocky jerk new person. Try and build up new relationships and new friendships. Remember how nice it was to have all that support from all your friends? You're going to have to develop a new "support" group where you are now.

Look, this is all very basic stuff that you probably already know, so I'm sorry for stating the obvious. I just want to cover as much as I can to be a help to you. Be patient with the "new" you. You've worked so hard to make these changes, now you get to live with them. Enjoy every minute.

If you have lost a lot of weight, don't walk around with your chest puffed up; be humble. Don't judge your friends who might be overweight.

If you're at your dream job or business, don't make fun of others who aren't. Remember what it was like to be where they are now. By now, you should be a little more mature than before, so all the petty stuff should be gone, right? I urge you again, enjoy it!

Truly enjoy radical change

You worked hard to get to this point; the process of getting here is probably still ingrained in you. Loosen up a little, and allow yourself to have some fun!

Remember we said we were supposed to enjoy the journey. Once we get there, we should take that enjoyment to level 10.

Be the carefree person you always should have been; be one of those people you used to meet when you took a vacation.

Don't let the old habits creep back in

One of the biggest dangers you have to watch out for, to always be on guard against, is that old habits will try to get back into your life. If you lost a bunch of weight, then watch out for getting back into eating junk food and putting the pounds back on. Once you get fit, watch out for the little voice telling you that you don't have to go to the gym anymore.

Once you have reached your new, fitter self, you don't have to work as hard as you did to get there, but you still need to maintain some sort of basic routine. If you have been doing these things all along, it shouldn't be too much of a stretch. Stick with the basics that you have already established and you'll be fine.

Really start to enjoy your exercise time; you can accomplish so much during that part of your life. Make it interesting; set little challenges for yourself, for example see how long you can run. You can also use the physical exercise time for reading and catching up on busy work. You don't have to work as hard as before, but watch out for laziness creeping back up on you.

Make sure you stay on top of your money

Money is one resource that you're going to need no matter what, so you have to keep a super-close eye on this one. Once you're truly living out radical change, you can develop a more laid-back mindset, and this might tempt you to be a little looser with the purse strings.

Remember what it took to raise the money to live out your dreams, and remember that you'll always need money to continue with your dreams. Keep saving, and keep your spending down. You have developed some great habits, so I know you'll be okay.

You already have the hard part down, so just maintain it. You know the drill. I don't want you to look at that nice stack of money in the bank and do something stupid. You're going to see all kind of things that you want, and with a stack of cash in the bank, you'll be tempted. Don't waste any money; do what you have to do, but don't be frivolous.

Watch out for negativity

Even if you move somewhere new, there will still be people you have to watch out for; you know how to handle these people. More than anything you must watch out for negativity in yourself.

We can so easily hate ourselves for something we did or didn't do; sometimes we have to tell ourselves to just shut up.

When you start to hear that doubt about being able to continue, that doubt telling you that you're dreaming, ignore it. Tell it to go away. It's not going to feel natural to you to be living out your radical changes, and sometimes it will seem like a dream. It's not a dream, and you worked very hard to get to this point. You deserve all the happiness and joy!

Say goodbye to the past and welcome your new life

If you are holding on to some old clothes from when you were bigger, get rid of them! That's the old life; embrace the new. If you want to keep one shirt to always remember, then go for it, but don't dwell on the past, and don't be introspective about your past.

When you first set foot in your new place, scream for joy. Do you realize what you have done? All your life you dreamed of certain things, and if you have followed through, now you have them. Don't plan on doing anything that first day, it's your day to relax and adjust. If you have a family, soak it up together. Run around the yard and be free.

You may not have lost weight, you may not have moved, your radical changes may be something completely different. Whatever they are, however you have changed your life, take the first day to really enjoy every minute. Even if you feel like your changes weren't that "big," you still have accomplished so much. Don't let anyone or anything put you down. Be proud of yourself.

I have to be honest and tell you I'm working on this journey along with you, but I can tell you that when we reach this point as a family, we will "live" that first day and the ones after.

We will live it up!

That's what this is all about, working hard at *living not just existing*, getting over whatever issues have stopped us in the past. It's about creating a step-by-step plan and finally taking action, and once we get to this point, it's all about enjoying it.

Yes, watch out for any old habits creeping up, but let's be honest . . . you got this.

We're here at the end of the eighth step, and we are finally living out radical change, what's next?

Chapter 9:

Chapter 9:

Pay it Forward

(Ninth and Final Step)

This book has given you a plan or guide to radically change your life, but I have to confess something. My goal for this book, and for the radical changes you and I and many others are making, is to start a movement.

I'm sure you've heard the saying "with great power comes great responsibility." Since we have learned and grown and changed, it's our responsibility to spread the word and help others. Why?

As humans, we always want to know what we're going to get out of something. Do you want to know what you'll get from helping others? You'll get to help change the world! Remember the inscription in the introduction:

are you LIVING or existing?

When I was young and free and my imagination
had no limits,
I dreamed of changing the world.
As I grew older and wiser I discovered the
world would not change –
So I shortened my sights somewhat and decided to
change only my country,
But it too seemed immovable.
As I grew into my twilight years,
in one last desperate attempt,
I settled for changing only my family, those closest to me,
But alas, they would have none of it.
And now I realize as I lie on my deathbed,
if I had only changed myself first,
Then by example I might have changed my family,
From their inspiration and encouragement I would then
have been able to better my country,
And who knows, I might have even changed the world.

This is an inscription on the tomb of an Anglican Bishop in Westminster Abbey.

This is so true, and now you have started the process by changing yourself. You have been down this road, you have sweated and planned and cried and been happy and experienced every other emotion you can think of. Now you see how we can change the world together.

Now I'm assuming that you have either said yes and completed your journey for radical change, or that when you're done with this book, you will start your path. If you think I'm a crackpot and aren't starting anything, then I wish you good luck in your life endeavors.

If you're with me, you understand fully what we need to do, and here are a few ideas to help us start this movement to radically change the world:

Chances are there is something you're really passionate about; it might even be one of the things you have radically changed or want to change in your life.

For me, what I'm passionate about is radical change and truly living, for you it's...

How much do I believe in your passion? There are a lot of different and maybe even scary things going on in our country right now, and a lot of people are looking to our government to solve their problems. Let's bring it a little closer to home; maybe you have been looking for something or someone else to help you with your problems. After reading this book, I pray you're not still looking for anyone else to solve your problems.

I understand that there are many hard situations out there that go way beyond what I understand, but I believe we have too many people looking and not enough people **LEADING**.

Maybe you have been looking when the truth is you should be leading. If you've made radical changes in your life, you definitely should be leading. So let's get back to that thing you're passionate about: we need you to lead us with your passion!

If you want to read something that will inspire you and explain this idea a lot better, read *Tribes* by Seth Godin. If you know right now what your passion is and how you should be leading us, I hope this book has helped give you experience with making changes.

I want to give you six points that will help you to start your movement.

Lead by example

No one will respect a word you're saying if you're not already living out your words. You've heard the expression that actions speak louder than words, and you know it's true. If you are to be our leader, we want to know that you're not a poser! The one thing that I hope you've learned from this book is to take action.

Lead with passion

You should be ready to scream what you're talking about from the rooftops and shout it in the street. That kind of energy and passion is contagious, and if you want to start your movement that passion needs to spread like wildfire. If the passion is not there, people won't believe in your movement; they'll assume you don't believe in it. It took great passion for you to get to this point, it took (or will take) passion to make radical changes in your life. You should be an expert on passion.

Convince people of the "why"

The best way to get people to join your movement is to show them why they should. When people focus on the "what" and the "how" they easily get discouraged and give up. When they can see "why" they want to join your movement, they will have the proper motivation to push forward and to push your movement.

Teach them that the movement starts from the bottom up, not the top down. What? Any movement starts with each of us as individuals. A great example is what Dave Ramsey is trying to do with his "Great Recovery" project. If we as individuals change what we are doing, then we'll change the whole system. If you're going to start your movement, it has to start fresh with each person. The "whys" will be the logs that get the fire hot!

Put boots to the ground

If you're going to start a movement, there has to be a point where you stop talking about it and start doing it. It's like the first point I made: people respect action, so give them some action. If you say you're going to do something then do it; always keep your promises of action and follow-through.

Don't give up! Even when it seems like no one else is joining the movement, don't give up! Even when it seems like no one else is listening, don't give up! Even when people make fun of you and think it's ridiculous what you're doing, DON'T GIVE UP!

It's time for all of us to wake up and start doing things that we are passionate about, things that matter, things that will make a difference in this world. As a Christian I believe the Bible, and in the book of Acts it talks about the twelve disciples of Jesus. After his death, they were hurt and kind of lost, but when they saw Him after His resurrection he gave them specific instructions. He started a movement that two thousand years later is still going strong. In the book of Acts, we see how twelve men turned the known world upside down with that movement. In the present day, I see how that movement has turned my life upside down.

You've come full circle

If you have gone through this journey (or will go through it), then I say congratulations. When you get to this ninth step you'll have a totally different outlook on life, a totally different attitude. As the last part of your transformation, give something back to someone who is a carbon copy of what you used to be.

Do you remember how it was for you? Do you remember the hopelessness you had? Why not go to that person and show them that it's not hopeless. Not only will you feel good, but you'll help start a movement that could change this messed-up world for good.

We're at the end of the book, and I want to encourage you, inspire you, and ask you to join a movement committed to radical change. The last part of this book is a call to action.

Will
YOU
Join Us?

Every movement starts somewhere, with at least one person. These people have joined me in this movement committed to radical change and changing this world for good.

David Constable

David is my little brother and part of my inner circle. He has worked at various "regular" jobs and has even worked for me in my bread business. David has decided the same-old same-old isn't good enough, and he is following his passion. He works at a traditional job right now, but he has a step-by-step plan to do what he really loves. His passion is to start a church in the inner city of Milwaukee; he also wants to start an online business to support him. Right now he has a website, which is the beginning phase of his journey: www.notforall30.com. Check out his website to see the start of his journey to radically change his life and the world. He has committed to this movement.

William Haeflinger

William at one point worked three jobs; he quit and came to work with me. He has been doing bread for the last six years but is committed to pursuing his passion: BBQ. His goal is to open a BBQ restaurant here in Milwaukee, with his own unique recipes. He has developed a general plan and is moving forward. William is committed to radical change and changing the world. You can talk with him here: www.facebook.com/william.haeflinger.

Chaka Dillon El

Chaka currently owns his own business, but music is his true passion. Chaka has written so much music, it just flows for him. He has worked many jobs and has been very successful, but it still isn't his passion. Chaka has committed to radical change and changing the world. You can find the beginning of his journey here: scientificmindsrecords.com. You can also find his music on iTunes, so go there and help him with his journey!

Kimanzi Constable (me)

I wrote about my story in my first book, so I'll give you the condensed version. I have worked at many different jobs some of which paid very well. I started a business, which at its height brought in $200,000 a year with four different guys. It was great money, but it's not and never was my true passion. I grew up a skinny kid, but after marriage put on some weight; at the time of writing this book, my weight was 300 pounds (ouch). I have discovered my true passion with work: writing. I have started my journey to radically change my weight; I want to lose 132 pounds.

I'm tired of not truly living life. In the end, I won't remember all the stuff I was able to accumulate because I made good money and bought all the "cool" stuff; I will remember all the experiences and the people that enriched my life.

I want to remember leaving the bad weather of Wisconsin to move to beautiful Hawaii.

I want to remember all the marathons I ran because I lost weight.

I want to remember all the things I did with my wife and kids and family because I didn't hold back in life.

I truly want to go for it and be tired at the end of the day from all the things we did.

Are you tired every day from all the things you did that just took your time, or are you exhausted from all the amazing things you experienced when you decided to live a life of radical change? I want that amazing kind of life. I have committed to radical change and changing the world. I even wrote a whole book about it!

You can find my journey at kimanziconstable.com.

In addition to the four of us, our families have committed to radical change and changing this world for good. So you're not alone! Fourteen people have already joined this movement.

Are
YOU
with Us?

If you want to join this movement or if you're committed to radically changing your life, let us know about it. Go to my website and declare it to the world: kimanziconstable.com.

Not only will it feel good, it will help you officially start your own personal journey to radical change. It will also encourage others to not be afraid and to take action.

Thank you so much for reading this book. Please help me spread this message by telling others to pick up a copy. You could also help me by going to Amazon and leaving a review.

Feel free to contact me anytime at my website, or email me and let me know how your journey for radical change is going.

Email me at kimanzi@talesofwork.com. I'd love to hear from and encourage you!

I would say good luck, but I know you don't need luck, you're taking action!

about the author

I'm thirty-two years old. I have been married to my wife, Tanya, for the last thirteen years, and I have two boys and a girl. At the time of this writing I live in Milwaukee, Wisconsin, but have plans to move to Maui, Hawaii, next year.

The move to Hawaii is what inspired this book. Read all about it at kimanziconstable.com.

I don't know about you, but I get tired of the "same-old same-old." Last year, I published my first book, *Tales of the Everyday Workingman and Woman,* which you can find at kimanziconstable.com. The book has done well and has inspired people everywhere to find their passion in their work. It also inspired me to pursue my dream of writing, which is what led me to the writing of this new book.

Is there anything in your life that you want to change? Do you know how? I was in the same boat as you; I did a lot of praying and soul-searching, and I decided enough was enough, it's time to live. If you're like me and have been going through life just existing, then I hope you read this whole book, get inspired to change your life, and pursue your dreams!

If you need help or want to talk one-on-one, email me at: Kimanzi@talesofwork.com

Or come by, get involved, and help others at kimanziconstable.com.

a little more
about the author

My Job

It was a cold and snowy morning and I was doing what I usually do at two a.m. every week day morning; I was wishing I was anywhere else.

I knew it was going to be a bad day when I got to the warehouse that morning and had to jump start the truck. Now to put this into perspective for you, I had to jump the truck with no light and the temperature was two degrees with a wind chill that made it even colder.

So as I got to the first store, I wasn't hoping for the best, but to be fair my everyday expectations with that job were not high. I was putting the second stack of bread (fifteen trays high) on the lift, and I could see things were looking sketchy at best.

I didn't trust my instincts and I went ahead and grabbed a third stack (what a dummy) and started to put it on the lift.

You see where this story is going, right? You're right; all three stacks fell right off and shortly after so did I!

So the day started out bad and went to horrible that fast. I was on the ground and so were three hundred loaves of bread that I still had to deliver and stock in the store.

This day was the tipping point for me, the day when I said enough was enough. I had thought about quitting this job every day for ten years, yet I had made every excuse in the book to stick it out.

I wanted to quit but didn't know how, didn't know what special skills I had or how I would support my family. My journey of discovery eventually led to writing this book.

My Weight

I don't know about you but I love food, I mean I'm literally a food junkie! When I got married I was a pretty skinny guy, but over the years a few pounds have been added on. Now I'm not saying it's because of marriage (I'm not blaming you my beautiful wife).

A few years ago my brother was getting married, and asked me to be his best man; I was a little surprised and honored. Everything was super exciting from the rehearsals to helping out with decisions for the wedding.

The bad part came when it was time to get fitted for the tuxedo and it was way too obvious that my love of food was showing. I tried on what I thought was my size, but quickly found out that food had won the war and I was now ten sizes bigger.

I was embarrassed and shocked by how much weight I had gained, but it didn't end there. The day of the wedding we were all at the church changing for the wedding and I had to struggle to put on my clothes. I got my pants on and needed pliers to get my zipper zipped!

Despite all of this, it wasn't the worst moment for me. That moment came weeks after the wedding when the wedding pictures came out.

I was excited to see the pictures until I actually saw them. In the pictures was when the reality of what happened hit me. I was horrified to see how much weight I had gained and how bad I looked, I literally started to cry.

You would think I should have realized that I had gained that much weight, but it didn't sink in until that moment. When I weighed myself on the scale that day (it had been years since I weighed myself) I almost had a heart attack when I saw that I weighed three hundred and thirty two pounds.

When I saw this I knew I had to do something about it. The changes were another part of the journey that led to this book.

Where I live

I was born and raised in Milwaukee, Wisconsin, and if you don't like the cold and snow, this is not the place for you.

When my wife and I first got married, we talked about moving out of Wisconsin and to somewhere warm that didn't get snow. We would watch all the TV shows about nice tropical places or houses that were right on the beach.

To make matters worse we took a vacation to St. Croix in the U.S. Virgin Islands and didn't want to come back. It was everything we dreamed about and more. We did come back to Milwaukee and we did settle back in, just settling for what we had; we were used to it.

One day we were late for work and when we got outside our cars were completely snowed in. We were both late and almost fired; that was the day we decided we had to get out of here.

You know how that goes right? We were all fired up and talked about moving to Texas, but didn't make real plans and let other people talk us out of it. We then went on a vacation to Maui, Hawaii and completely fell in love with it., we knew this was where we wanted to move. Making that happen has been another part of the journey that led to this book.

Radical change

These are a few of the major things that I wanted to change in my life, but I wanted more than that. I didn't want to change and fall right back to the same old same old. I wanted changes that would stick, changes that would last for a lifetime. I wanted a completely new life.

As I thought about how to make these changes I searched for books that could help me change my life. I was disappointed by what was out there. Since I couldn't find what I needed, I decided to come up with my own game plan, not only to change, but also to make changes that I knew other people would think were radical.

Aren't you tired of the seesaw ride, tired of seeing some success only to revert back to where you just came from? I wrote this book for myself, but also to help those others who desire real and lasting change. The decision to define and share what I was doing to create radical change in my life was the final step of the journey that led to this book!

This is a realistic playbook that you can use to make radical change. Discover the life you really want and deserve to live. That life is waiting for you, so read this book, use the step by step plan, and go for it!!!

radical changes

_____

_____

_____

_____

_____

_____

_____

_____

_____

_____

_____

_____

_____

_____

radical changes

_____

_____

_____

_____

_____

_____

_____

_____

_____

_____

_____

_____

_____

_____

_____

radical changes

---

radical changes

_____

_____

_____

_____

_____

_____

_____

_____

_____

_____

_____

_____

_____

_____

_____

radical changes

_____

_____

_____

_____

_____

_____

_____

_____

_____

_____

_____

_____

_____

_____

_____

radical changes

---

radical changes

_____

_____

_____

_____

_____

_____

_____

_____

_____

_____

_____

_____

_____

_____

_____

radical changes

_____

_____

_____

_____

_____

_____

_____

_____

_____

_____

_____

_____

_____

_____

radical changes

_____
_____
_____
_____
_____
_____
_____
_____
_____
_____
_____
_____
_____
_____
_____

radical changes

_____

_____

_____

_____

_____

_____

_____

_____

_____

_____

_____

_____

_____

_____

_____